I0617537

www.ingramcontent.com/pod-product-compliance
Lightning Source LLC
Chambersburg PA
CBRC0908441206226
46551CB00011B/752

About the Illustrator

Steven Kennedy has an MFA from San Francisco State University. His novel *Birds of Massachusetts* was published by Fourteen Hills Press in 2020. He currently writes about the San Francisco Giants for SB Nation's McCovey Chronicles.

84 Ways to Pray

People People Media Foundation
9998 Crow Canyon Road
Castro Valley, CA 94552

www.peoplepeoplemedia.com

84 Ways to Pray

Written by Jared Callahan
Illustrations by Steven Kennedy

felt incomplete. My religious experience told me that I should pray every day and while I tried mightily, I always felt like my prayers fell short. Sometimes I worried that I was simply bad at prayer. The primary modes of prayer I learned reduced God* to a heavenly vending machine. Still, something deep inside me whispered there was more.

As I began to experience different ways to pray, my formulaic approach to prayer quickly broke down. Participating in different congregations, cultures, and religious traditions caused me to revisit the practice of prayer itself. My stale prayer life became uncomfortable, yet this discomfort invited reflection, engagement, and action.

In over a decade of working with teenagers in church, I slowly developed a long list of ways to pray. Through presentations, seminars, and conversations, this list grew and grew. The list expanded to include the details of my own prayer experiments, suggestions from others, and foundational prayers from a variety of Christian and other religious traditions.

This project is not a comprehensive explanation of prayer. This book is a generative brainstorm that expands how prayer can look, feel, sound, and be.

a set-aside time of devotion, prayer can be incorporated into everyday life. Regular actions can become worshipful. Many daily routines can be transformed into moments that turn our hearts toward gratitude, justice, and deeper love of God* and neighbor. Prayer can be daily habits, creative practices, embodied experiences, meditations, internal musings, group activities, and guided reflections. These different ways to pray can carry us across various spiritual seasons. As we grow personally and our external circumstances shift, we can allow our experience of prayer to evolve to match who we are becoming.

My intention for this project is to provide space to deepen your experience of prayer. By gathering together a variety of approaches to prayer, I invite you to engage prayer as a practice. There is no expectation for perfection, but rather an opportunity for growth. I hope you learn new ways to pray, transform ones that no longer serve you, and even add to the ever-growing list, so that this 84 Ways to Pray community can learn from you.

May you encounter goodness and transformation as you fumble through ways of prayer that are new to you.

- Jared

*God

Oof, a small word that means so many big and messy and mysterious things. The word "God" carries some heavy baggage.

The Hebrew word for God was written incomplete, translating to "G-d." The point being that the concept of God itself is too big to be contained within a single word or human language.

So, when we say "God," we acknowledge some things we can name and so many more that we cannot. God, Holy One, Love, Creator, Redeemer, Sustainer, the Flow, Mystery, The Divine Dance, Lord, Allah, Abba, Healer, Most High, Everlasting One... G-d.

What is prayer?

Prayer is reaching in
and reaching out.

Prayer holds sacred all parts within yourself, deeming them worthy of acknowledgment. Then prayer serves to lift them up, outside of yourself. It shares these thoughts, feelings, reflections, and inclinations with the God with whom you are in relationship.

Prayer is connection. Prayer is devotion.

Prayer is a practice that takes practice.

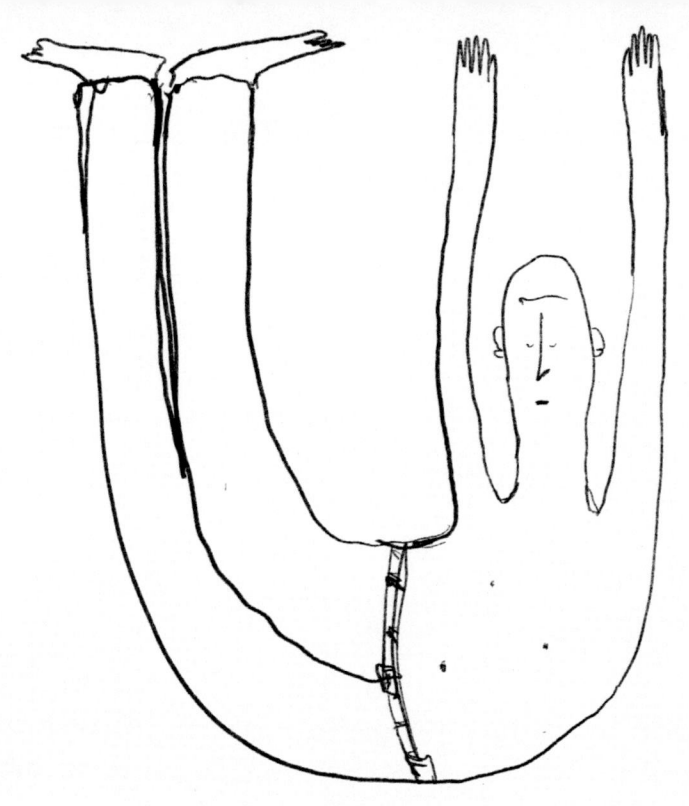

Love is a choice.

Love is unselfish.

Love is a commitment.

Love is a covenant.

Love is refined by challenge.

Love is hard for me to accept from God.

Love is something I want to work on.

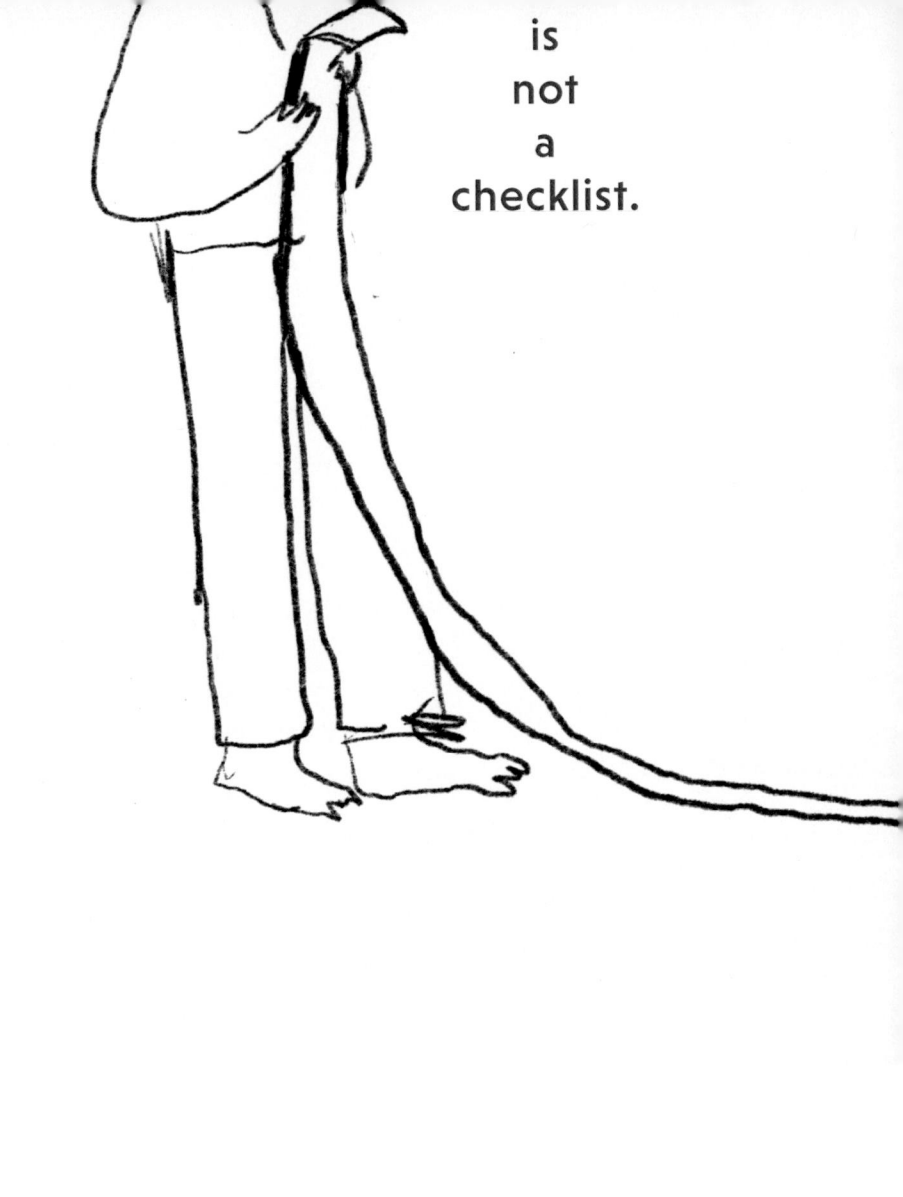

is
not
a
checklist.

An easy temptation would be to turn this book into a list to accomplish. I beg you not to rush through. Please resist our culture's lie that you can have everything you want, to the fullest extent it exists, immediately. We know this to be false, yet try anyway.

We cannot have it all.

This is a lifetime's worth of material. You're invited to try a new prayer practice every week, month, season, or even year. The ones that you are not initially drawn to or do not particularly enjoy might end up being the most transformational. Take it slow and steady. This is not about winning anything. Just slow and steady.

Practice rarely makes perfect.

Perfect is bullshit, and not the goal of prayer anyway. Give yourself grace and recognize the ways that the journey changes you. The only way to fail is to ignore the lessons that these practices have to teach you. The point is the journey. The journey is the point.

Here we go...

Listen

Carve out time to be away from the noise and pace of regular life. Silence can be painful. Recognize your ego (your "monkey mind") trying to keep you from silence. Name it and set it aside. Recognize and release. Silence and stillness will never just happen; they are the byproduct of work, of resistance.

This honestly might be the hardest one in the book for me. Everything wants our attention. Lean into the stillness. Start small. Battle for silence. Finding it is an activity; it will never happen passively.

Breathe

Breathe slowly and intentionally. Listen to your breath, slow it down. Inhale for four seconds, hold for four seconds, exhale for four seconds, and wait to inhale for four seconds.

Breathe in something you know to be true.
Breathe out a distraction.
Breathe in God's truth.
Breathe out a worry.

How can we be both so big and so small at the same time?

My ideal place for this is feet in a creek or standing near a body of water. If not that, a room when you're home alone works great too.

This is a great place for the "Fuck You, God!" prayer.

Nothing we say to God can threaten God. In fact, I reckon the most honest thing we can do in relationship with an entity claiming to be all-powerful is to express honestly all of our thoughts and feelings. This prayer provides the perfect place for anger, and also gratitude.

Hold Others in the Light

Quakers use the language of "holding people in the Light."
Pause, take a deep breath, focus on the person in need, and
invite them to be covered in God's Light.

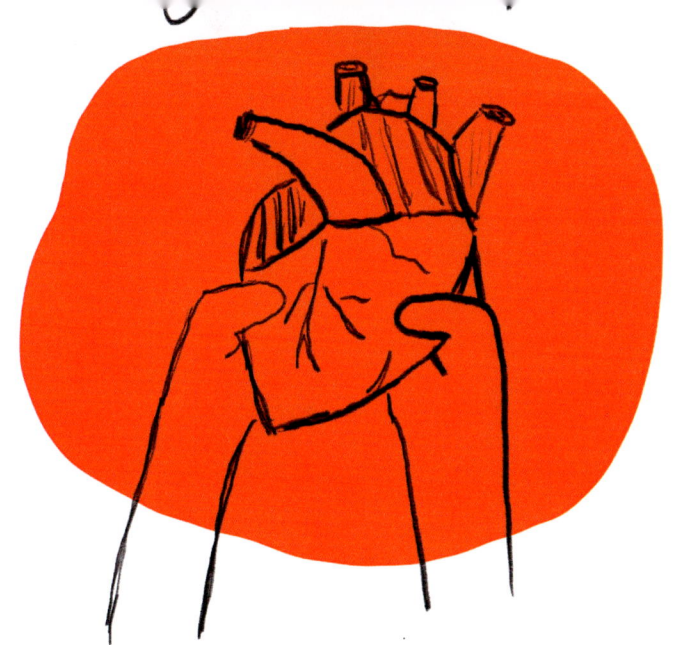

This is gross.

Common Prayer

(Yes, that's a picture of a book within a book)

Transformational prayers have been collected for centuries, gleaning from the wisdom of the ages. These countless prayers from religious texts and spiritual communities are available to you and me to guide our current prayer sessions. Written prayers connect us to the body of believers who proceed us and to the population of people who pray around the world today.

It may seem like cheating by praying someone else's words, but there is immense value in praying prayers already prayed before.

These prayers have provided structure for me in many seasons when I didn't feel like I had anything original to offer, or couldn't find the words to say. The prayers that have been used by the Church for generations are often taken directly from Scripture or written by historical pillars of faith. These prayers put words to the deep thoughts and feelings that I am trying to express and often lead me to parts of my spiritual journey that I have not yet encountered.

One of my most transformational guide prayer experiences came through practicing Ignatian Spirituality. I participated in a year-long experience that incorporated different spiritual exercises, prayer, contemplation, discernment, spiritual mentorship, and the Prayer of Examen. The Prayer of Examen is a structured daily reflection that opens us up to recognizing the divine presence in your day.

A Guided Prayer:

Breath Prayer

This prayer originated as "The Prayer of the Mind" and is credited to monks in the Egyptian desert in the early 4th century.

The simple yet potent content focuses my mind. The repetition brings me back when I wander.

Pray the first line as you inhale and the second as you exhale. Repeat it as you breathe.

Detach

The Buddhists have a foundational teaching: the cause of all suffering* is attachment. If I can constantly acknowledge and relinquish my way, then I might be present in every moment, including my own death.

What does it mean to accept that you're going to die?
How does that help you detach? Where does your focus go?

What is suffering?

Any time we are not in control.[1]

At its broadest, suffering is anytime we are subjected to circumstance. It's part of the reason traffic can enrage someone so quickly. When we leave destination A to head toward B, we never account for all the things that can go wrong while driving. Every obstacle is an affront to our authority and autonomy, which moves us to feeling hurt (which is often followed by hurting someone else).

Fast

Fasting is intentionally abstaining from a common behavior for the sake of spiritual devotion. When your habitual impulse takes you toward the item or action you are fasting from, you can use that as a reminder for prayer.

Common fasts include, but are not limited to, food, beverages other than water, social media, etc.

Fasting is the great unused spiritual discipline in the United States today. In a culture so focused on consumption as a means of happiness, fasting points us towards true joy, through gratitude for what we have and a focus on the needs of others.

I acknowledge there is tension in recommending "going without" to those who might already be without, not by choice.

Also, I'm not a doctor.
Research facts about the health of fasting and speak with your healthcare provider. I recommend the BBC documentary "The Science of Fasting" if you're interested in learning more.

Take a Shower

Before starting the water, get in the shower.
Already standing in the path of the water, turn the faucet on.

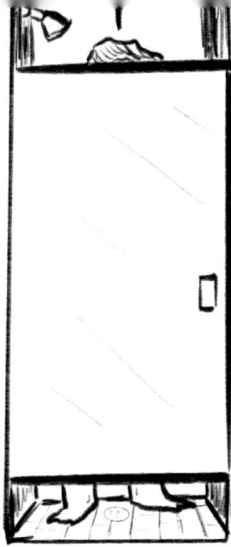

Medical Daily reports cold water showers being good for immunity, circulation, weight loss, stress reduction, muscle soreness, and depression.[2]

And you get used to it.

Often, the water will have warmed up by now, and
you'll appreciate the luxuries you do have.

Shower shorter and save water.
Also, pray for those without access to clean water.

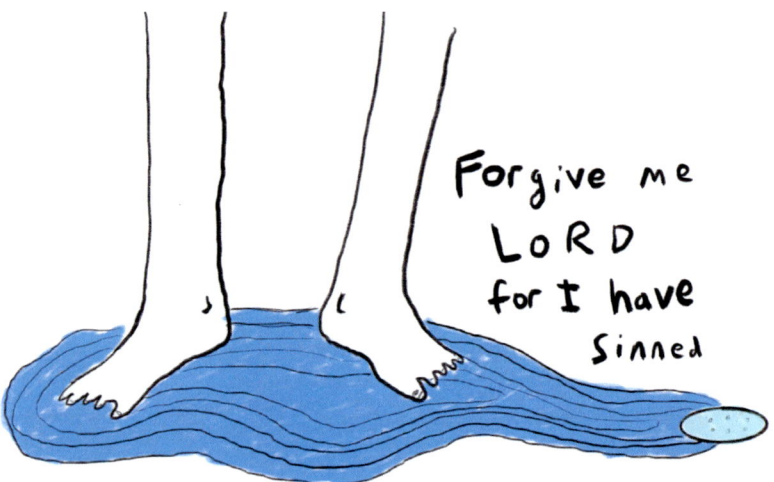

In the winter, the water can literally be freezing cold. Use a five gallon bucket, collect the freezing water, and then use it to water plants or do dishes. Hop in when you can tell it's beginning to get warm.[3]

I always thought sin was "disobeying a known law of God." Now, this is not tons of flaws for me. Reflect on that definition for even a minute or two, and a number of solid "what if" questions can slowly erode that statement.

One.

Later in life, I was offered an alternative definition: "Sin is anything less than perfect love." In true Jesus-style, it opens up the definition and breaks down my propensity toward scales of badness and us/them language. It replaces small-minded pebble counting with lofty, holy aspirations that every thought, word, and action can be the most loving.

*Repentance

*Reconciliation

Repentance comes from the same root word as "to turn around." It literally means to go in the other direction. Admitting the damaging act is the first step. The second is to go in the other direction.

Reconciliation is the rebuilding of relationship after annihilation. Often, through the hard work of forgiveness and reconciliation, a relationship has the ability to become stronger than it was before the original wound.

Drinking water is the recommended way to wake up. We are supposed to start our days by drinking large amounts of room temperature water. Use that time to pause, thank God for sustenance, provision, and for your body today.

Water Plants

Pray for the ways that God can be growing you. Pray that God would give you eyes to see your progress and patience for where you're not yet developed.

A routine practice like watering plants is an opportunity to worship. Especially if you are using your cold shower water.

Brush your teeth

Pray that God will use your words to participate
in the reign of God on Earth.

Bathroom Bonus:

A friend recently told me about reading Scripture while brushing teeth. I left a Bible with a bookmark on the bathroom shelf.

You'd be surprised how much you can read in the two minutes it takes to brush.

Try not to drool.

Use a Singing Bowl

This is a type of metal bowl people ring in moments of prayer and meditation for its calming tone produced by the vibrations. Sometimes known as Tibetan or Himalayan bowls, they have been used for centuries, particularly by Buddhist monks.

Our farm community uses the singing bowl to mark our times of communal prayer. The repetition of the bowl provides a soothing way to enter and exit a time of vulnerable intentionality in prayer.

Make a Prayer Canvas

Get an art canvas of any size. Use pens of different colors to write out the prayers of your heart. When I did this, I left my canvas on the floor, leaning against the outside of my closet. At the beginning or end of my day, I'd plop down on the carpet and write. Over time, it provided a way for me to see the ways different prayers had been answered over time. I started a new canvas for every year.

I started pasting scraps of paper, scribbled notes, pieces of church bulletins, photos of people, and any other random thing that needed lifting up. You can slide extra heavy paper things (or things you don't want others seeing) into the back seams of the canvas, or tape them on the back.

Fun fact: Bowing down before someone originates in the time of swords and kings. Bowing to a knee and lowering your head was submitting to authority because you were giving them the "kill shot" — the opportunity to slice the back of your neck: If they allowed you to rise, every breath of your life from that point forward was because they had allowed it.

How does this shift what it means for you to kneel or bow your head in prayer?

Men have been removing their hats as a sign of respect or adoration since medieval times. It is suspected to have started as a way of revealing your true nature to the person you are greeting. You couldn't hide your true identity beneath a mask, shield, or hat if it was removed voluntarily.

Why do we fold our hands?

Similar to bowing our heads, it is suspected that putting our hands together was a sign of submission, i.e., being ready to have your hands bound by an authority. Today it would be akin to being handcuffed. This is a reminder that Christianity developed as a sect in persecution during the Roman Empire.

A lot is happening when we take off our hats, bow our heads, and fold our hands to pray.

Yup.

Build an Altar

In the Bible, the people of God built rock altars to commemorate significant moments during which God moved amongst them. Future generations got to see the rocks and tell stories to remember the faithfulness of God.

"Then the Lord appeared to Abram and said, 'I am going to give this land to your offspring.' And Abram built an altar there to commemorate the Lord's visit."

Genesis 12:7

Use a Prayer Stool

At Taize, a monastery in France, all the monks use these small wooden prayer stools. After a bit of kneeling in prayer, your legs will fall asleep. The small stools support the weight of your body in a way that keeps your back flat and knees protected.

You can buy the stools from the monks, which is how they pay to keep the lights on and food on their table. Or, you can make them. My church had a work day and everyone made two: one for themselves and one to leave in our communal worship space.

Forgive

It seems to me that Jesus' most difficult commandment is to love our enemies.
Forgiveness is so countercultural, so anti-logical,
that Jesus deems it a holy action.

Attempting to forgive is prayer itself.

Try forgiving someone. See what happens.

Prayer honestly acknowledges our whole selves: the parts we are proud of and the parts we try to hide. Sometimes the best way to engage in prayer is through sharing this with others, who often reveal God's love to us.

How can God know me better? Everything I've ever been taught is that God knows everything about me (my deepest thoughts, the hairs on my head, my actions before I do them, etc.). I did some soul searching and figured out that I have some different layers of self that I reveal to different people. If Level 1 is common stuff, and Level 2 is my thoughts and beliefs, then Level 3 is the deep stuff I hide from others (and maybe even myself).

Sharing these parts of myself is a vulnerable experience that leads me into deeper healing and connection. Through meaningful conversation, I often come to know myself and others better and thus become more capable of love.

You are invited to use these questions in prayer and/or in small group conversation.

Which encourage you? Which are difficult to engage? Why?

4. What is the deepest joy you have ever experienced?

5. When do you feel misunderstood?

6. What is your deepest passion in life?

7. What hurdles are you currently facing?

8. What is God teaching you right now?

9. What is your life's purpose?

10. If you died tomorrow, would you be proud of your life?

11. Who has wounded you most deeply in your life? Most recently? Have you forgiven them?

12. What's an aspect of your family of origin that you want to carry forward?

13. What's an aspect of your family that you want to leave behind?

14. What do you regret?

15. What's the one question you were hoping wouldn't be asked of you? Answer that question.

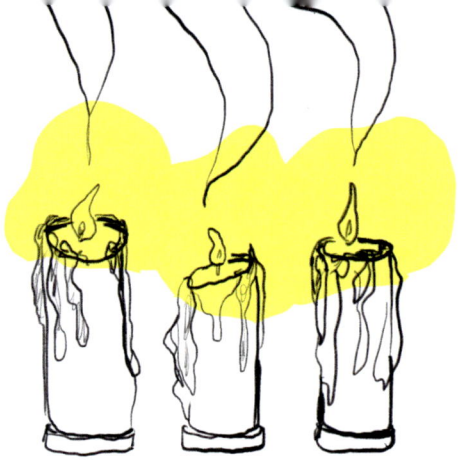

Light a prayer candle or incense

People of faith have been lighting candles in prayer for thousands of years.
As your regular actions resume, the heat, smell, and smoke of the candle are
continually lifted up to God.

Bonus: Light a candle in a pitch black room. Watch how far the light goes. Watch it
dance. The tiny light is powerful in darkness.

This is often done as a guided experience that leads you in an imaginative prayer exercise to build a dwelling place for your inner self to spend time with God.

The goal is to imagine a space that holds all thoughts, feelings, memories, shame, and hopes. God is invited to dwell within a space built by all that you are. My practice is finding God in the prayer mansion and saying what needs to be said, or listening to what needs to be heard.

Once you've been to your prayer mansion once, you can visit by yourself anytime you'd like.

For me, this prayer practice has wildly grown over the years, as I often discover new rooms and spaces in the house. My space is near a forest with a creek and a swimming hole. It has a big porch, and lots of complex rooms where different pieces of myself dwell. When I visit it in my imagination, it is interesting to sit in the lobby and sense what area God might be waiting to speak with me in. The room for forgiveness? The kitchen? The study?

Confession:

Often, it feels like I get to the Prayer Mansion and enter a room that God has just left. It feels like the story in Exodus 33:19-23.

The Lord said, "I'll make all my goodness pass in front of you, and I'll proclaim before you the name, 'The Lord.' I will be kind to whomever I wish to be kind, and I will have compassion to whomever I wish to be compassionate. But," the Lord said, "you can't see my face, because no one can see me and live."

The Lord said, "Here is a place near me where you will stand beside the rock. As my glorious presence passes by, I'll set you in a gap in the rock, and I'll cover you with my hand until I've passed by. Then I'll take away my hand, and you will see my back, but my face won't be visible."

Commute

Lift up the people whose houses you drive by, or the people who are brought to your mind by the things you see. I love reading street names and praying for the people in my life with those names.

Scroll

Let social media remind you to pray for the people you are following.

Follow people with a different worldview, especially those with whom you disagree. Pray for patience and empathy as they express their worldview publicly. How does their reality influence your reality?

We should all make more things that have no end goal,
ther than to take us on a journey.

What is art?

To be art, a piece must have complexity, subtlety, and originality.[5] Art exists within a conversation about what has been done and the times in which it is being made. Art has something to say.

The process of creating is what is valuable. The practice of making the piece allows you to forge a pathway that will be ready to process weighty stuff as it arrives. Often art is fed by suffering and doubt. It engages the weight of life and channels it into healthy expression. Along with other steps toward health, your habits of creativity can vulnerably transform traumatic experiences into fertile material for change in yourself and in the world.

B ody

L abors

E motions

S ocial Life

S alvation

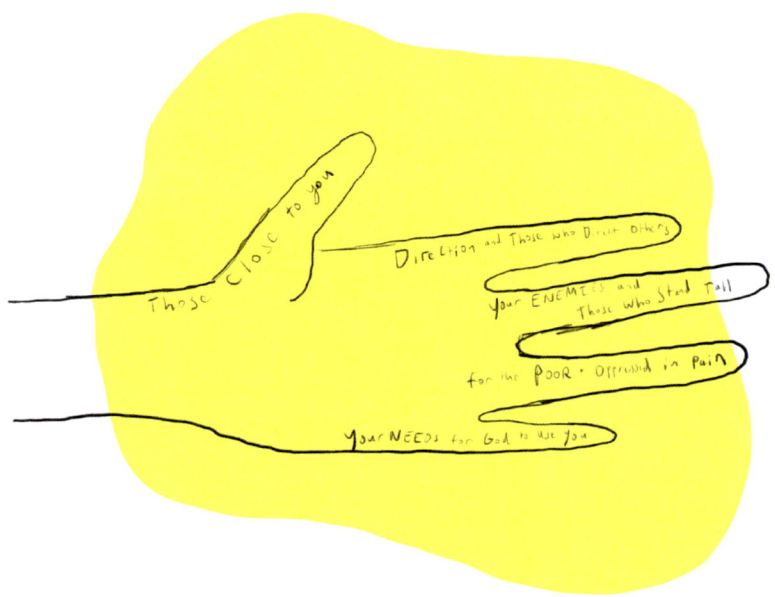

Those Close to you

Direction and Those Who Direct Others

Your ENEMIES and Those who Stand Tall

for the POOR · Oppressed in Pain

Your NEEDS for God to use you

After all, the German phrase "gesundheit" has become a common response to sneezes, and it literally translates to "To Your Health!" We often pass on a blessing without recognizing it.

Pray in Tongues

Depending on your religious background, you might have a varying degree of understanding and experience with speaking in tongues. Speaking in tongues is a gift of the Holy Spirit given to some who call out to God in a holy groan with meaning indiscernible to most other humans. To someone unfamiliar, it sounds like praying an aggressive mumble, or like parseltongue in Harry Potter.

There are a couple practical stories about speaking in tongues in the Bible. The Holy Spirit allowed the disciples to speak the native tongue of the people they were ministering to.

DOVE!

Speaking in tongues is considered a gift with which the Spirit is able to take our deepest heart issues before God without the limitations of human language.

If you are interested in praying in tongues, consult with someone with experience. I have participated in a couple of prayer sessions where I was led in praying in tongues.

I have experienced others praying in tongues multiple times, but I have never personally prayed in tongues as a genuine expression of prayer.

Whew. Humans are messy - so simple and yet so complex. God is both simple and complex. Humans have messed up so much. Reading through, I realize how many of these concepts were taught to me through the thick layer of others' motivations and received through the thick lens of my own current worldview.

I'm sorry for any spiritual abuse you have endured.

My hope is that prayer transforms the hurt I've received and perpetuated, thanks to the abundant love and grace of God.

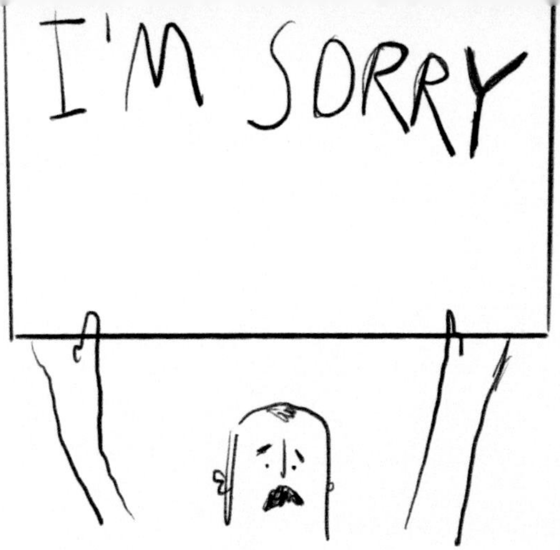
I'M SORRY

Pray for Healing

I have some friends who pray for healing and see people healed in front of their eyes. I have some friends who pray for healing and have never experienced any miraculous events.

My friend Dan was dying of ALS. People prayed for him to be healed. He prayed for his own healing. His thoughts: "God invites us to ask for healing. I'll continue to pray for healing. It doesn't mean God doesn't love me if it doesn't happen."

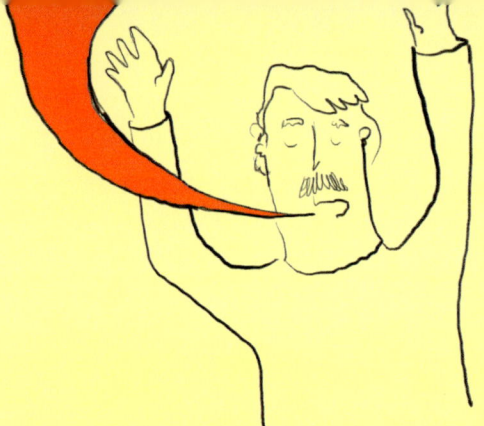

"When you pray, don't be like hypocrites. They love to pray standing in the synagogues and on the street corners so that people will see them. I assure you, that's the only reward they'll get. But when you pray, go to your room, shut the door, and pray to your Father who is present in that secret place. Your Father who sees what you do in secret will reward you.

When you pray, don't pour out a flood of empty words, as the Gentiles do. They think that by saying many words they'll be heard. Don't be like them, because your Father knows what you need before you ask."

Matthew 6:5-8

WARNING:

Jesus calls out praying in public for people to see. Instead, Jesus encourages listeners to go pray to God in private.

This passage seems to be about the heart of the person praying. If you're praying to receive the praise of other humans, then you've received all the reward you'll get.

Practice the Prayers of the People

When hosted in a group, this practice can give space for individuals to pray out whatever they want. It can be a word, a sentence, a praise, or a request.

This has proven to be very engaging for people who were once terrified of praying aloud in the presence of others.

The individual prays, then says:
"These are the prayers of my heart."

The group responds aloud:
"Lord, hear our prayers."

There is unifying power in a community praying through a list of concerns, at the same time.

Have someone prepare a list in advance and either read a topic aloud every 30 seconds or advance through a slide deck.

Sample:
Our anxieties
Our joys
For grace and peace
Our families
This group
This block
Our schools
Our co-workers
Our community
Our city's marginalized
Our city leaders
Our state's marginalized
Our state leaders
Our country's leaders
Our country's enemies
The Earth

Hold Something

Many religions use counting prayers with tactile strings or ropes for guidance. A Catholic rosary serves as a physical guide through a variety of sacred prayers. Holding a tactile object while praying connects the physicality and movement of our hands touching with our brain and soul pursuing God.

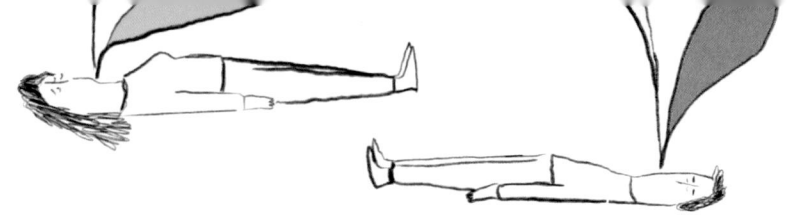

Call and Respond

There are a variety of written prayers in which a leader says a line and the group replies. These are often practiced on Sundays, during certain seasons, while receiving communion, or for special services in the Church calendar.

My in-laws attend a Christmas Eve service every year with a small countryside congregation. I married into this tradition, and the first couple of years, I missed the meaning of the service by focusing on fitting into the holiday family dynamics. However, after years passed, I realized the congregation was following the same service order every year. This included the songs, Scripture readings, and prayers. At the end of the service, every attendee would light and hold a small candle, and this prayer was led. When I allowed myself to be fully present, this prayer greatly moved me, and has since spent years taped on my bathroom mirror:

Blessed are you, Prince of Peace.
You rule the earth with truth and justice.
Send your gift of peace to all nations of the world.

Blessed are you, Wonderful Counselor.
ou enlighten the heart with steadfast love.
**Enliven your church that it might bear good
tidings of great joy to all people.**

Blessed are you Emmanuel.
You promise to be with us even to the end of the age.
**Open our eyes to see you in all who are
hungry, lonely, or homeless.**

Blessed are you, Son of Mary. You share our humanity.
Have mercy on the sick, the dying, and all who suffer this day.

Blessed are you, Son of God.
You dwell among us as the Word made flesh.
**Reveal yourself to us in word and sacrament that we may bear
your light to all the world.**[8]

Read the Psalms

Pick a passage in Psalms and read it out loud.

The Psalms in the Hebrew Scriptures provide a fantastic breadth of experience. I was raised thinking they were exclusively flowery songs, but in fact, a significant portion are lament psalms. To lament means to mourn. To express grief, heartbreak, and sorrow. Knowing that, reading a psalm as prayer can provide entrance into a heartfelt prayer over thousands of years old. Often, a psalm committed to memory will pop back into your head when it is needed most.

Pray the A.C.T.S.

This was the first structured prayer I was taught. It gives an easily memorable structure to ensure our prayers are well-rounded, as mine can easily slip into being lists of "wants."

Adoration
Confession
Thanksgiving
Supplications

New resources seem to be popping up every day. Ask someone you trust
for a recommendation, or start with one of these:

Pray as You go
Calm

If you need a place to start, author Phyllis Tickle compiled multiple books on praying the hours that are organized by season in the series *The Divine Hours*.

As I cruised around on my rollerblades doing my paper route, I imagined Jesus skating along with me. As I proudly drove my first car, I imagined Jesus in the front seat, listening to music loudly and always being willing to listen if I remembered to talk. This helped me immensely, because praying to "nobody" wasn't encouraging me to pray.

Set an Alarm

For years, I had an alarm that went off at 3:20pm. It was a reminder to pause, read/recite Ephesians 3:20, and pray for 30 seconds that God would do more than we could ask or imagine in our community.

Ephesians 3:20-21 (CEB):
"Glory to God, who is able to do far beyond all that we could ask or imagine by his power at work within us; glory to him in the church and in Christ Jesus for all generations, forever and always. Amen."

Alcoholics Anonymous was founded in 1935, and from the beginning has had participants focus on the existence of and relationship with a higher power. A different prayer is attributed to each of the Twelve Steps.

I had the privilege of working for a couple years with men in a residential recovery facility. One of the men shared a little note card containing pocket prayers, which included the Third and Seventh Step's prayers in recovery. He said that having these prayers always at his disposal connected him to the community. Committing these prayers to memory can prove to be wildly useful.

The Serenity Prayer has been used in recovery groups since the 1940s. The abbreviated version may be familiar to you:

"God, grant me the serenity
to accept the things I cannot change,
the courage to change the things I can,
and the wisdom to know the difference."

-Reinhold Niebuhr

Can we recognize the season? What does it mean to name the winter (or fall, spring, or summer, for that matter)?

Spending time in nature reconnects us with the cycles of the earth. I have found it incredibly beneficial to work on a farm, grow food in a garden, swim in a body of water, and spend time in the trees.

Ever-loving and holy God,
Hallowed be your name.
Your reign come, your will be done,
On earth as it is in heaven,
Give us this day our daily bread,
And forgive us our sins, as we forgive those who sin against us,
And lead us not into temptation, but deliver us from evil,
for yours is the reign, and the power, and the glory, forever.
Amen.

In *Prayers of the Cosmos* by Neil Douglas-Klot he translates the original Lord's
Prayer text written in Aramaic as:

O Birther! Father-Mother of the Cosmos,
Focus your light within us – make it useful:
Create your reign of unity now
Your one desire then acts with ours,
As in all light, So in all forms.
Grant us what we need each day in bread and insight:
Loose the cords of mistakes binding us,
As we release the strands we hold of other's guilt.
Don't let surface things delude us,
But free us from what holds us back.
From you is born all ruling will,
The power and the life to do,
The song that beautifies all,
From age to age it renews.
I affirm this with my whole being.
Truly power to these statements –
may they be the ground from which all my actions grow.
Amen.

Catholics make the Sign of the Cross for many reasons, including proclaiming a miniature symbol of their faith, marking their process of emulating Christ, and renewing their baptism.[9] It is a simple action that carries profound meaning.

To perform the Sign of the Cross:

Touch your forehead with the end of your
two fingers and thumb and pray,
In the name of the Father

Move your hand to the middle of your chest and say,
and of the Son

Move your hand to the left side of your chest and say,
and of the Holy...

Move your hand to the right of your chest and say,
Spirit.

the Son

touch chest

the Holy Ghost

touch left
then right breast

Pray with Icons

For over 1,500 years, icons have been used to illustrate numerous stories and people from religious texts and convey theological meaning. Before reading was common, detailed images invited the population into understanding various scriptural narratives. Icons also include saints or respected faith leaders.

Praying with an icon means being present with and taking in the image as a portal toward divine connection. Time spent with an icon can lead to reflection and response. Continued meditation with an icon can lead to rest and experiencing God's presence. Icons are seen as windows into the Holy.

If you want a place to begin, spend time with the icon of Christ Pantocrator, Rublev's trinity, or Julian of Norwich. Also, a great Instagram follow is artist Kelly Latimore Icons. He paints various cultural, political, and religious figures in iconography style.

Sing Songs

Songs can provide an accessible way to put deep thoughts or feelings into words. You can write an original song, or trust a song that puts Scriptures or prayers to music.

Try singing prayers in public.

This one caught me really off guard. My partner and I committed to joining the staff of a small residential church. We traveled to visit them and ended up at lunch. After the server took our orders, the group just started singing their prayer over the food.

We were in the middle of a trendy lunch spot. The whole patio stopped talking and listened. When we finished, there was a moment of pause, and then the regular sounds of a restaurant began again. No one clapped, and no one booed.

Our singing prayer served as an interruption in our quest to fit in.

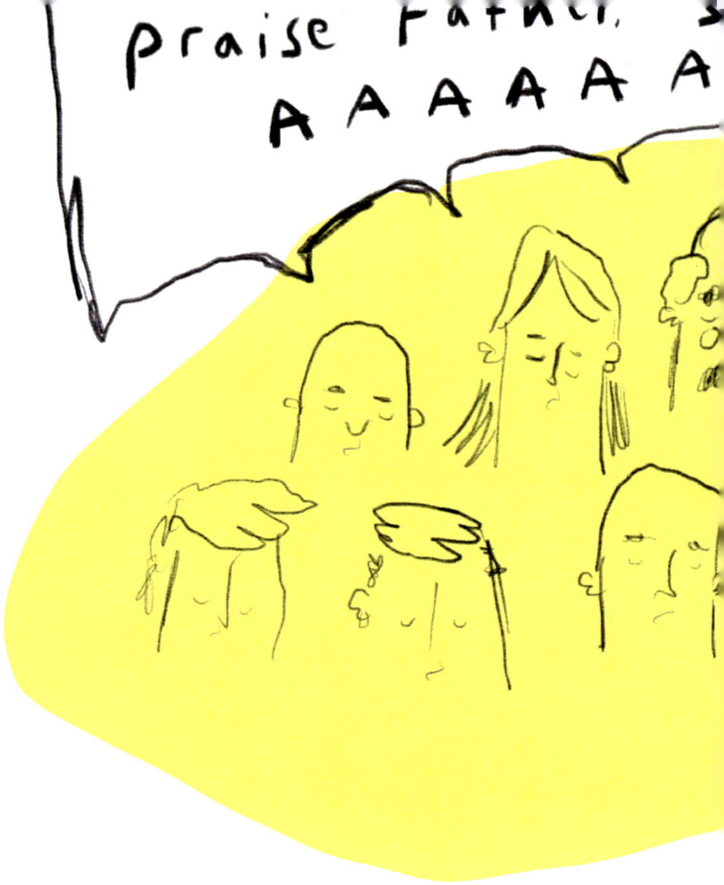

praise Father,
AAAAAA

Prayer can provide a welcome interruption to the repetition of normality. When we can practice prayer that challenges seamlessly fitting into a self-focused narrative, the disruptions to the routine help us recognize holy moments around us.

Many of the predominant messages we absorb daily are that we are "not enough" or "incomplete."

Using God-focused language helps remind us of our true identity as God's beloved in a larger story.

Food is holy.

My American culture has shaped me to believe that food should be fast, fatty, and easy. It can merely serve as fuel to do, do, do more.

However, because it requires constant contact with the Earth, food provides multiple daily opportunities for deeper connection to where the food comes from, who provides/prepares it, and what it means to our bodies. Working on a farm, I am constantly humbled by the seasons and cycles of the land's production, the care needed by the trees, and the slow time the food needs to grow. Preparing food brings people together and teaches us about culture, seasoning, spice, temperature, and time.

Food is the opposite of the immediate.

Let the deliciousness of food that you eat remind you of God's goodness. Also, pray for those without food and people/organizations that provide food.

COME to the **TABLE**

The early church ate meals together, and while they'd eat, they would participate in the Eucharist, or communion. When we take the bread and wine (or grape juice) in remembrance of the life, death, and resurrection of Jesus Christ, we pray with our minds and bodies.

We engage communion every week at our table church meal. Approaching the table weekly as a community resets our priorities to our commonalities, as average relational tensions regularly consume our thoughts. Having to encounter an invitation to existence on a deeper plane can be both challenging and refreshing.

Pray over your purchases

Engaging this area as prayer, rather than a mindless participation in consumerism, causes ripples of transformation. We can review the way we spend on home items, clothes, investments, everything, as a practice of prayer.

Ask yourself: Does this dollar I am spending participate in God's reign of Love on earth? Who am I affecting with this purchase? What am I supporting?

I use Better World Shopper as a guide to inform me about the companies I patronize. This process felt exhausting at first, but soon I figured out which brands were more ethical, and have never gone back. It gets easier, and it has been so worth it.

See way #1 on listening. How are we so busy and full of content that we don't have space dedicated to silence, listening, and waiting on God? Can chores be a space of listening?

Let the innocence of a pet remind you that God looks at us the same way.

Resist Injustice

We are praying when we engage in protest, resistance, and action against all forms of oppression and injustice.

This journey has revealed to me ways that I am the oppressor, which leads me to apology, repentance, and alliance. As you unearth areas in need of change, be strengthened by prayer and encouraged by a community standing alongside you to bring about liberation.

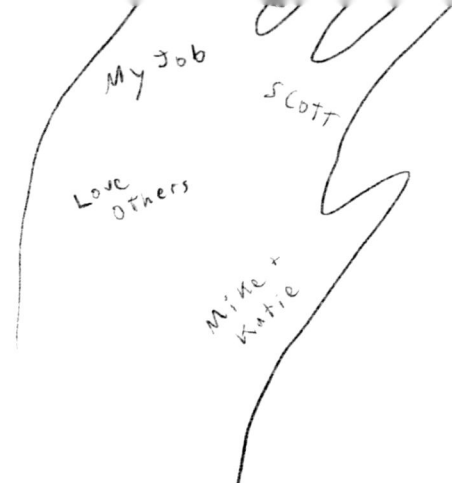

Prayer became a regular thing in my life in my early twenties when I started writing prayer requests for others on my hands in pen. I'd always see my hand, and the constant reminder of the needs of others provided meditative moments for me.

Problem: I had a prayer I wanted to remember during the day, but the request itself was sensitive.

(This is a real prayer of mine.)

Get a tattoo as
a reminder to pray

Dance

Have you ever seen an incredible partner dance? My wife dances, and she sees things in dancers I would never notice. Even my untrained eye has the ability to sense when dancers transcend reality through dance. It is a holy blend of practice and trust, expression, sharing, and communion.

The divine dance is the best picture of the Triune God's relationship with Godself, and what we are invited into. Dance around! Pray your favorite song, sing out. Cut loose. Dance like no one is looking.

Make Something by Hand

The act of creating something new is an inner journey that becomes expressed outwardly. There are countless new connections to discover within and around ourselves when we make or observe something new. Making things makes me appreciate things made by hand.

In many religions, God is considered a Creator. We are invited into co-creating with God. Creating by hand is participation in God's ongoing creativity.[10]

I've often felt that having my feet washed is more difficult than washing someone else's feet. Why is that?

Walk

Walk around a neighborhood with the intent to pray for the people, places, and situations God brings you to.

If you hike or run outdoors, try turning off the music or podcast, and praying through your exercise. Praying while moving provides a perfect time to listen.

Ask for Prayer

For a season of my life, I found myself in church groups where someone would ask, "Does anyone have any prayer requests?" Then, silence... no one would say anything! Eventually, someone would request something trite to fill the silence. But we can jump on those opportunities! Lead with vulnerability. I realized that there are always tons of different things I could be asking my community to pray for.

I've started trying to request prayer. If you are with people who profess religious beliefs, then go for it! Or, go for it anyways? I find that the sum of a lot of religious people hanging out does not often produce something overtly spiritual. Although this can totally be fine, I recognize that I've probably become too comfortable with not bringing up Jesus. I want to be the kind of person who gets to learn about the journey of others, and I miss out when I'm not confident enough to bring it up.

Walk at Night

The world has a different volume at night.

One night, I stepped out onto the local road that roars with traffic during the day. But at night, there wasn't a car to be seen in either direction It was surreal and serene.

*Don't get hit by a car, otherwise you might need someone to...

Look at Your Newsfeed

Let the scrolling content remind you to thank God for the healthy aspects of the world, and lift up to God the ways that you still need God's peace, patience, healing, and deliverance.

Pray over the current events trending on your newsfeed.

Also, follow social media and check the headlines from the major news outlet not of your natural persuasion. Following multiple flavors of news is humbling, infuriating, and always draws me back to prayer.

Pray the Scriptures

Pray God's promises back to God. God is God. If God said things through the authors of the Scriptures, it's a reliable prayer method to pray God-language back to God.

Pray for Social Issues

Every time someone is killed in the United States by the death penalty, I mourn and pray. I picture Mary weeping at the foot of the cross as she lost her son to capital punishment. I pray against racist and biased systems. I pray for the innocent whom we've incarcerated and whom we have killed.

Lord have mercy, Christ have mercy.

Confess

Practice confession to a trusted friend or family member, pastor, or priest. Confession moves things weighing you down from inside of you to outside of you. Admitting these things to another person smashes their control over you and is a major step toward health and healing.

One of the great untapped aspects of humanity is the freedom that comes from confession, repentance, and reconciliation. We have the ability to remove the power from the secret by bringing it into the light.

Pray through physical activity

I had never considered this until my brother said he works out to thank God for the gift of his body.

This was a revelation, because I had considered my body wholly separate from my spiritual life. Upon reflection, so many of my prayer practices are embodied. Prayer is active.

This doesn't mean comparing our bodies to others, but being in tune with the vessel we inhabit. How can we be kind to ourselves? How can the upkeep of our bodies be worship?

TIME

OUT!

Pause

Pause when you're insulted, offended, or angry - Pray in that moment. Why are you angry? Is it zeal? If so, catch your breath and defend the defenseless. Are you proud or insecure? If so, lay out your heart before God, be forgiven, and then forgive and move forward.

Embrace Interruption

This is a tough but fruitful way to pray. So many great stories begin with vuption. But personally, I can't stand interruption. I am always surprised how fast I can go from monk to assvhole when something gets in my way. That anger is always hovering just below the surface. Embracing interruption as an opportunity to be present and abide in peace participates in kindom* on earth.

*Kindom

I recently learned the colonial roots and traumatic connotation of the word "kingdom," which had been used in my religious upbringing. "Kindom" serves as a substitute that focuses on kindred relationship.

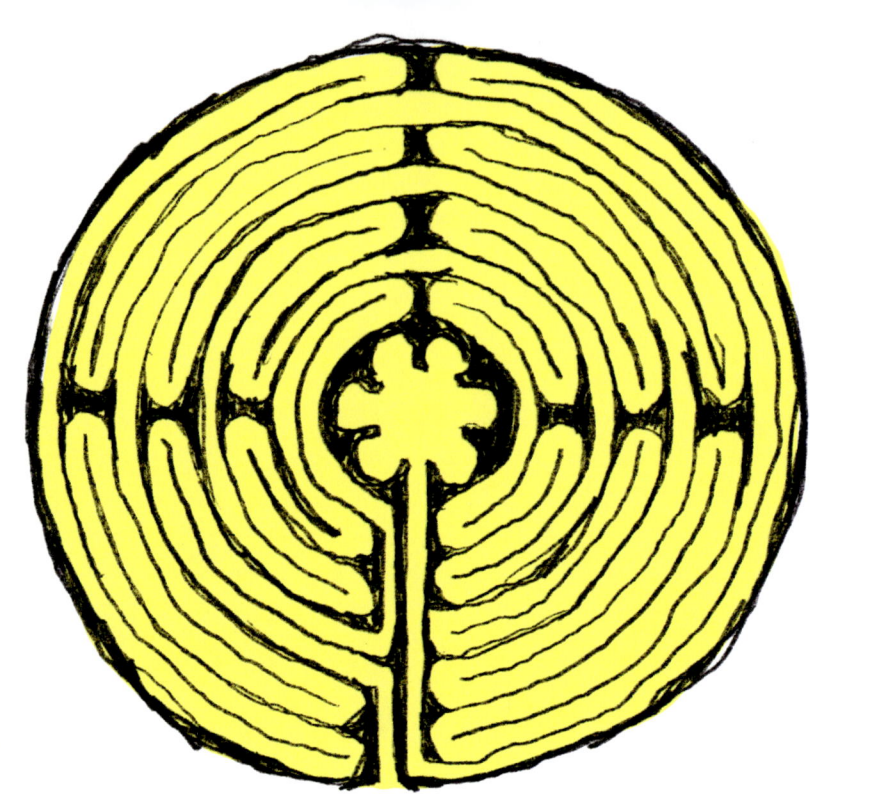

Pray Your Worries

Turn them over to God. Hold an object like a rock, name your worries, and release the rock.

You'll be surprised how much emotion can come out when you name your rock with the things that trouble you. I have cussed out a rock, cried over it, and then dropped it back amongst the rocks. Or, bonus: throw it into a forest or a body of water.

Use Everyday Reminders

Designate everyday occurrences that remind you to pray (e.g. passwords, commercial breaks, seeing Palm trees reminds you of Palm Sunday, etc.)

I learned this from my dad. For twenty years the password on his work computer was a prayer reminder. Way to go Dad!

What are things that remind you to pray?

Do a Weekly Review

Weekly examination of conscience provides space to reflect on the highs and lows of a week gone by.

Pick a regular time to pull out your journal. Answer these questions:

What have you done that made you feel fully alive?

What were the highlights of your day?

Have you experienced anything lately that robbed you of your joy?

Imagine yourself
in a story from Scripture

Read the story. Close your eyes and picture yourself as a
different character in the story.[11]

For example, in the story of the woman at the well in John 4, be:

Jesus
The woman
The disciples
The well
The townspeople

How does that bring Scripture to life?
How does that change the way you pray the story?
How does it change what God might be saying to you?

"If any of you are sick, they should call for the elders of the church, and the elders should pray over them, anointing them with oil in the name of the Lord. Prayer that comes from faith will heal the sick, for the Lord will restore them to health. And if they have sinned, they will be forgiven. For this reason, confess your sins to each other and pray for each other so that you may be healed. The prayer of the righteous person is powerful in what it can achieve."

James 5:14-16

Anoint with Oil

There are a number of stories in the Bible where the characters put oil on the head of a person being dedicated for holy work. The Hebrews used it exclusively for prophets and kings, which is why the New Testament stories regarding the use of oil are so inflammatory. Oil is used on Jesus, and oil is used on the sick in prayer. The use of aromatic healing plants is symbolic in declaring someone set apart, holy, or pure.

Prayer Journal

Keep a journal tracking what you are praying for. As time passes, re-read what you've been lifting up. Go back and fill in when prayers have been answered or how your request has been transformed.

There is a rabbinical saying that we "walk backward into the future." While we cannot see our future, we can see how God has been faithful on the journey thus far, which gives us wisdom to move ahead.

Teach me please!

So, I got to way to pray #84 and just couldn't stop.
What are other ways you pray that I haven't experienced yet?

Share with us @84WTP
or #84waystopray

Further Reading

"A Prayer Journal" Flannery O'Connor

Common Prayer: A Liturgy for Ordinary Radicals (pocket edition)

Mary Oliver

Philis Tickle

Wendell Berry

4. "You must be doers of the word and not only hearers who mislead themselves. Those who hear but don't do the word are like those who look at their faces in a mirror. They look at themselves, walk away, and immediately forget what they were like. But there are those who study the perfect law, the law of freedom, and continue to do it. They don't listen and then forget, but they put it into practice in their lives. They will be blessed in whatever they do." James 1:22-25 CEB

5. Art critic and theorist Libby Lumpkin coined these parameters

6. Love to Pray—A 40-Day Devotional For Deepening Your Prayer Life by Alvin Vandergriend

7. Written by Cardinal Bergoglio (before he became Pope Francis)

8. Lutheran Book of Worship

9. https://www.simplycatholic.com/six-reasons-why-we-make-the-sign-of-the-cross

10. This illustration is an homage to Man Ramp and Worble. We love their vibe and want to give credit where credit is due. Shred on.

11. This is an Ignatian spiritual exercise founded on the life and writing of Saint Ignatius of Loyola. I participated in a yearlong group prayer led by an Ignatian teacher. It was transformative, and I'd be wise to participate again.

12. The CEB Study Bible. Edited by Green, Joel B., Common English, Common English Bible, 2013.

I owe all that I am to the communities that have shaped me. Thank you to my family, childhood church, university, San Diego First Church of the Nazarene, colleagues, friends, farm, and filmmakers.

My deep gratitude to Jeff and the Heirloom East Bay intentional community for your faith in action. Spending this season living and working on a farm has rewired my connection to God, myself, others, and the land.

Thank you Steven, Natalie, and Rachel for gifting your incredible talents to creating this book. I hope countless people can engage prayer in new ways because of your work.

Thank you Sophie. Your way with words combined with your deep spiritual quest make my unending brainstorms combined with unbridled enthusiasm into something valuable.

Jet, Milo, and Murphy for being my crew.
You are truly wonderful humans... and a cat.

About the Author

Jared Callahan co-founded a farm-based intentional community in the hills south of Oakland, CA. His film work has screened at over 200 film festivals and debuted on The New York Times, GQ, The Atlantic, and PBS. He loves walking in the creek with his two sons.